O9-ABI-905

Serving the
Children
of the World

Caring for the Earth

Let's Reduce Garbage!

by Sara E. Nelson

Consulting Editor: Gail Saunders-Smith, PhD

Consultant: Kate M. Krebs
Executive Director, National Recycling Coalition, Inc.

Capstone press
Mankato, Minnesota

Pebble Books are published by Capstone Press,
151 Good Counsel Drive, P.O. Box 669, Mankato, Minnesota 56002.
www.capstonepress.com

1 2 3 4 5 6 11 10 09 08 07 06

Library of Congress Cataloging-in-Publication Data
Nelson, Sara Elizabeth.
    Let's reduce garbage! / Sara E. Nelson.
    p. cm.—(Pebble Books. Caring for the earth)
    Summary: "Simple text and photographs describe ways for children to reduce
their garbage and why it's important to do so"—Provided by publisher.
    Includes bibliographical references and index.
    ISBN-13: 978-0-7368-6324-7 (hardcover)
    ISBN-10: 0-7368-6324-9 (hardcover)
    1. Waste minimization—Juvenile literature. I. Title. II. Series.
TD793.9.N45 2007
363.72'8—dc22   2006005417

Note to Parents and Teachers

The Caring for the Earth set supports national science standards
related to conservation and environmental change. This book
describes and illustrates ways children can reduce their garbage.
The images support early readers in understanding the text. The
repetition of words and phrases helps early readers learn new
words. This book also introduces early readers to subject-specific
vocabulary words, which are defined in the Glossary section. Early
readers may need assistance to read some words and to use the
Table of Contents, Glossary, Read More, Internet Sites, and Index
sections of the book.

Table of Contents

Too Much Garbage!

Andy throws away
lots of garbage.
Do you know
where it goes?

Some garbage
is taken to landfills.
Many landfills
are getting full.

Ways to Help

Jake's mom buys him toys with little packaging. This reduces garbage. Then Jake does not have much to throw away.

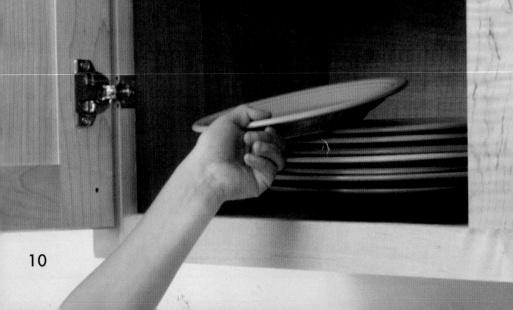

Paper plates
are disposable.
They are used only once.
Missy washes dinner plates
and uses them again.

Durable items can be
used over and over.
Ann will use
her backpack for years.

14

Many items have
lots of wrappers.
Bob's family buys items
with fewer wrappers.

Some items come in
many small packages.
Emma wants one big item.
Then she will reduce
her garbage over time.

Caring for the Earth

Matt teaches people
how to reduce garbage.
Then less garbage
will go to landfills.

We can work together
to take good care
of the Earth.
Let's reduce our garbage
to keep Earth healthy!

Glossary

disposable—made to be used once and then thrown away

durable—made to last for a long time

landfill—an area of land where garbage is placed and then buried

package—a carton, box, or case that holds something; food, toys, and other things you buy often come in packages.

reduce—to make or use less of

Read More

Bedford, Deborah Jackson. *Garbage Disposal.* Action for the Environment. North Mankato, Minn.: Smart Apple Media, 2006.

Galko, Francine. *Earth Friends at Home.* Earth Friends. Chicago: Heinemann, 2004.

Internet Sites

FactHound offers a safe, fun way to find Internet sites related to this book. All of the sites on FactHound have been researched by our staff.

Here's how:

1. Visit *www.facthound.com*
2. Choose your grade level.
3. Type in this book ID **0736863249** for age-appropriate sites. You may also browse subjects by clicking on letters, or by clicking on pictures and words.
4. Click on the **Fetch It** button.

FactHound will fetch the best sites for you!

Index

Word Count: 141
Grade: 1
Early-Intervention Level: 15

Editorial Credits

Mari Schuh, editor; Juliette Peters, designer; Wanda Winch, photo researcher;
   Scott Thoms, photo editor

Photo Credits

Capstone Press/TJ Thoraldson, 4, 8, 10 (both), 12, 14, 16, 18
Photodisc, 20
Shutterstock/magri, cover; Tonis Valing, 1
The Image Works/David R. Frazier, 6

Capstone Press thanks Jean Lundquist, waste management specialist in Blue Earth
County's Environmental Services Department in Mankato, Minnesota, for her
helpful assistance with this book.